Dedicated to all who do Hospital Chaplaincy and speak words and a word of healing to their patients .....

FOREWORD :

Words are important; our world is filled with words used to communicate - meaning, attitude, emotions and intent? Words and more words; every space in the world of ' instant communication ' we have now is filled with words and more words? The words used a lot of the time do not have much meaning, concern, emotion or weight behind them? I guess we have all heard about ' sound bites '. A lot of our words are just for instantaneous reaction and are ' sound bites ' in themselves? They are given more for effect rather than having any long - term meaning and significance attached to them?

With words we use; we can plant, uproot (much like the commission given to the Prophet Jeremiah) or even start fires in people's lives who hear our words? The power of words can be seen in the simple reality of the power of both the words themselves and the tone of voice they are delivered in? Think about the effects on both children and animals of your tone of voice? Low and soft tone of voice is appropriate for both and when used in relation to both groups it does not provoke? But rather allows one to communicate freely to both groups? This is just one example of how words and their use by ourselves can be important; it is multi - faceted and not just about the words or word used itself?

In the New Testament in the Gospel of John 4 : 46 - 54 Jesus Christ has an encounter with a Royal official. His use of words and a word of healing are profound and worthy of note and an attempt to understand? Jesus Christ vocalizes the word of healing and the official's dying son is healed and brought back to life. The very word and words of Jesus Christ have power and authority when it comes to the healing of the Royal official's dying son? The man's son is restored to life out of death and in the end the whole household of the man comes to believe in and accept Jesus Christ?

John 4 : 46 - 54 CEB .

" He returned to Cana in Galilee where he had turned the water into wine. In Capernaum there was a certain royal official whose son was sick.

When he heard that Jesus was coming from Judea to Galilee, he went out to meet him and asked Jesus if he would come and heal his son, for his son was about to die.

Jesus said to him, " Unless you see miraculous signs and wonders, you won't believe".

The royal official said to him, " Lord, come before my son dies".

Jesus replied, " Go home. Your son lives." The man believed the word that

Jesus spoke to him and set out for his home.

   While he was on the way, his servants were already coming to meet him. They said, " Your son lives! ".

   So he asked them at what time his son had started to get better. And they said, " The fever left him yesterday at about one o'clock in the afternoon."

   Then the father realized that this was the hour when Jesus had said to him, " Your son lives ." And he and his entire household believed in Jesus.

   This was the second miraculous sign, Jesus did while going from Judea to Galilee."

1. Healing by words or a word?

I have spent 13 or 14 years working as a Hospital Chaplain in a number of Hospitals. One of the things you learn in this profession is the power, impact and effect of your own words over both yourself and your patients. Words are very important tools of communication in our Global village of today. Think about how most wars and conflicts in the Global Village have their origin in miscommunication and the misreading of emotion, intent and purpose behind the words used? This is *true of countries, two individuals, two nation - states and even two people groups? Words are important and their use can have such a force and impact; it is therefore important we care about how we use the very words and word we vocalize? Mainly because we have a myriad of examples in the Global Village when they are misused and miscommunication happens and takes place?*

One of the very real things we learn as a Hospital Chaplain is that your conversation full of a variety of words with a patient can and does have a very real impact upon their physical well -

being. We can speak life or death into people we speak to. The research on patient outcomes with spiritual support in terms of Chaplaincy would support this contention. Words are so important; the very words we use and the tone of our voice can be and is so important in the Hospital context. One can speak life and positive medical outcomes into patient's lives in this context. In this context and many other contexts our words can and do have very real impact and effect and effects upon people who hear them?

Yet even in our everyday lives our own words have and can have the power of life and death over people's lives and situations? I am not thinking about positive thinking or belief. Rather I am focusing on the very speech full of our words we use to communicate ideas, concepts and feelings and emotions to others? Our speech can have and does have very real effects and impacts upon individual's we know and communicate with in; in our various world's? Just imagine and picture in your mind's eye; you speaking positive things into a person's life and imagine them smiling and laughing and receiving your words positively .... It can be so easy to cut down and wound with our words. ... What if we used our words to speak life, health, healing and hope into somebodies else's life? All of which is why the Word of God is so strong on our need to really think about our tongues, speech and our words and word. We really do have the power in that small organ inside our mouths to tear down or build up or wound without hope of any healing?

As a Hospital Chaplain I have had the opportunity over and over again to speak a word or *words in a particular season of a particular individual's life. Over and over again after visiting Hospital patients I would find myself wondering and reflecting on why I had said such a word or words to patient X? People have long talked about words or a word in season but this is especially true in the profession of Hospital Chaplaincy. There was always the opportunity to say a kind word but I am envisaging and throwing the concept of a word having much more impact and effect rather than just kindness? The times I am reflecting upon were when the words or word I spoke into a patient's life that had a visible effect and impact upon both their physical, mental and even spiritual health?*

I specialized in aged care Chaplaincy; this concept of a word or words in season is particularly true when dealing with the mature - aged? Also more specifically when dealing with those who have dementia. Again and again you can have the opportunity to speak a word or words in season that will really resonate with them? The word or words in season may well have a real impact and at times did in bringing them back into the so - called ' real world '? The word or words may well trigger a memory they have about their family or what they used to do as a job? All of which may well reconnect some of the neural pathways in their brains; leading to a better health outcome for them?

The title of this chapter is healing by words or word and I believe that healing can come from our word or words? It can also be assisted and aided in an individual's life and circumstances by our own very words and word that we use as we relate and interact with them? Communication of *healing; the possibility of and expectation of it can be and is so important to both communicate and believe in at the same time? Words and a word can be and are so important in relation to healing; particularly when they are in season and relevant to an individual's life and circumstances?*

2 . Verse 50 " Jesus replied, " Go home. Your son lives." The man believed the word that Jesus spoke to him and set out for his home". The word of Jesus Christ was enough for the Royal Official to believe in?

For the Royal Official to believe that his son would be healed and the word of Jesus Christ was enough to make that happen? The interesting thing to note is that the official wanted Jesus Christ to physically come to his dying and bring healing to him. He believed that is only

Jesus Christ would go with him to his sick son; his son would be healed. He has heard stories and whispers about the carpenter from Nazareth who had brought healing to many. Now his son was gravely ill and sick; he wanted some of that healing power to be brought to bear upon his son's condition and illness?

The interesting thing to understand and note is that Jesus Christ does not actually fit in with the plans and desires of the official? Even when Jesus knows fully that the son is very ill and near death? Out of this comes the understanding that Jesus has the power and authority over sickness and illness and can bring healing? Yet conversely He does not always fit in with us in our needs and wants for the spectacular healing?

I believe in the reality of supernatural healing for today....I have seen too much positive evidence and evidences of it in my years as a Christian not to believe in it and the One whose power and authority is on display in it? Healing does still take place and there is much that is not acknowledged as healing and supernatural healing at that?

The other interesting thing is that Jesus Christ speaks and vocalise's the word and command of the healing of the official's son? No bells, smells and incantations used but rather the word of healing pronounced over the official's son's life by the Son of God Jesus Christ? I believe that we need to be guided by the Holy Spirit in situations where healing and supernatural healing is required by an individual ....It may *well be that the Holy Spirit has us command in the name and authority of Jesus Christ of the person? When one is led to do this it is in the power and authority of the Father, the Son and the Holy Spirit that one is doing it and whose power and authority is being shown? The reason this is being stated very clearly is because I and you do have or possess the power and authority to bring healing and supernatural healing to a person? I guess that is why the healing is called supernatural because it is outside the bounds of what we would normally expect to happen with a person who is ill?*

An example and illustration from my own life will hopefully throw some light on the points I have been trying to make thus far? About 25 to 30 years ago I was in Perth, Western Australia to attend an evangelistic event for the America's Cup in WA. I went one night to an evangelistic crusade and at the end the preacher wanted to pray for the sick. The preacher said if you had an illness put your hand on that part of your body? I had a cogential defect in my right lung which affected my breathing ....

All I did was put my hand over my right lung and held it there as the preacher prayed for people. He prayed out aloud for the healing touch of Jesus Christ to come upon people in the auditorium who had sickness, disease or illness in their bodies.

Weeks later I had to have an x - ray as part of my medical assessment for something else and they could find no deformity in my right lung? The deformity in my right lung had gone and I had not even known it was gone? At the time of the preacher's prayer being uttered in Perth I sort of believed and had a small amount of faith in my healing. So when I discovered the deformity was gone my faith, belief and thankfulness to God was there. Like Jesus in John 4 all the preacher did was command and speak the word of healing. God the Father, the Son and the Holy Spirit did the healing and brought it to bear on the deformity in my right lung? Again it was showy, pushy or even spectacular and yet the healing of my right lung did take place? A friend of mine has kept the x -rays that prove the reality of the healing of my right lung that night at the crusade in Perth, WA.

Both in my own personal experience and that of the Official in John 4; we both had to do something once the word of healing had been prayed or spoken? In my case the action was putting my hand over my right lung as the preacher prayed for the healing of people in the auditorium? In the case of the Official it was actually believing in the word of healing spoken and commanded by Jesus Christ. He had to believe it enough to go on his way back to his home and his son?

He trusts the healing word and command of Jesus Christ enough to begin the journey home to his dying son? The Official did not just have a belief, faith or wishful thinking on his part, he showed real belief and trust in that he was prepared to accept and receive and even believe the word of healing by Jesus Christ for his dying son? My own belief would be that he would not have even begun the journey home to his son without Jesus Christ unless he trusted the word of healing from Jesus?

The Official had originally wanted Jesus to physically accompany him back to his son; so his son could be healed by Jesus Christ. So therefore we see a remarkable shift in the desire, emphasis and intent of the Official as he comes to accept the word of healing for his son spoken by Jesus Christ. He now believes the word of healing uttered by Jesus Christ. Jesus Christ no longer has to be physically present with him and be with his son for the healing to take place? The word and command of healing by Jesus Christ regards his son is now enough for him to be satisfied with and believe in?

The word and command of healing by Jesus Christ were spoken personally to the Official regarding his son. It was spoken personally to the Official; there was a personal encounter and word and command from Jesus Christ that formed the basis for the healing of the Official's son? Jesus Christ made the healing of the Official's son personal and gave it His personal touch through the word and command of healing given?

In the end because of what had

happened with the son the Official and his entire household come to believe in Jesus Christ. Therefore; for him and his entire household it becomes a thing of personal faith in the reality and truth of who Jesus Christ was, is and will be? His whole household come to have faith in Jesus Christ as the Christ, Messiah and the Son of God. All of which is not a given textually in the passage but that is what is at stake in their household coming to faith in Jesus Christ? The personal command, word and touch of Jesus Christ seems to make all the difference in the situation of the Official and his household ....

3. " Jesus said to him, " Unless you see miraculous signs and wonders you won't believe." Jesus said this to the Official and then does the very thing He is saying He does not want to do?

Sometimes I guess we can tend to be like the Royal Official and have need of miraculous signs and wonders before we will put our faith and trust in Jesus Christ? Or may well be it is simply we will not choose to believe until we see miraculous signs and wonders done by Jesus Christ?

Some always want the miraculous signs and wonders and they can go into a state of denial if they are not forthcoming?

Throughout the Book of the Acts of the Apostles, signs and wonders followed the proclamation of the Gospel message by the Apostle's and the faith communities they had formed? Signs - wonders + proclamation of the Gospel = Faith in Jesus Christ - salvation coming to an individual or community? Throughout the New Testament the miraculous signs and wonders done by Jesus Christ and the disciples and Apostles who operate in His name were done to generate faith and belief in Jesus Christ?

Sometimes in our modern contexts of the Global Village sadly we have cleaved a massive gap between signs and wonders and the proclamation of the Gospel? This observation would appear to be true of our proclamation of the Gospel and sharing of it particularly in the West and the contexts of Western Civilizations?

The enlightenment has

much to answer for and one of those things is the way it promoted reason and thought above the supernatural signs and wonders done by God the Father, the Son and the Holy Spirit? For me this is when the great divorce between Gospel proclamation and accompanying miraculous signs and wonders occurred?

Do not hear me decrying our use of reason or our minds but at times we theorize and paint ourselves into a corner where we simply cannot believe in the miraculous signs and wonders; even of the New Testament? My question is if it is the same *God and the Son of God we are still worshiping and serving why do we believe it cannot happen today and in our generation in the Global Village? At times we desperately want to do the cut and paste version of the New Testament devoid of any form or inkling of the miracles or even miraculous signs and wonders? These miraculous signs and wonders might offend our intellectual and reasoned belief and faith and our sensibilities attached to both?*

I love that God the Father and Jesus Christ and the Holy Spirit can and do ask us to use our minds? But if in that use of reasoning and intellect we fail to comprehend the totality of God regards miraculous signs and wonders; is it of any value?

Knowledge and reason can and does of itself puff up an individual and make and can make them have even an intellectual pride in the face of Almighty God? There is an arrogance that will not allow for the reality that God the Father, the Son and the Holy Spirit can and do in - break in supernatural ways into our world and its history everyday?

For me one is committing intellectual suicide if one believes; basically that God can no longer do miraculous signs and wonders as done in the New Testament era and epoch? The God of our imaginations and the one we can construct with all our knowledge and reasoning can often be far smaller than the God of both the Old and New Testaments? My whole hearted belief is that I always need to allow the God of the Word of God to be truly the God of the Word of God?

At times it is like we put handcuffs on the God we supposedly worship and serve and tell Him that He is not allowed to do anything out - of - the - ordinary; the so - called miraculous signs and wonders? Mainly because we cannot rationalize these away and deny the God who is behind them and His Glory, power and authority? He is who He is and He is allowed to do anything He wants to do and that includes the miraculous signs and wonders. You can probably tell that I am not a cessationist? I believe that miracles and miraculous signs and wonders still take place in our time and era in the Global Village and its history? Proclamation of the Gospel = signs and wonders and faith in Jesus Christ ?

Jesus Christ, the Father and the Holy Spirit do not have to always produce the miraculous signs and wonders for belief and faith in Jesus Christ to happen and occur? Yet with some individual's it is the very miraculous signs and wonders that some us decry that bring them to point of belief and faith in Jesus Christ? To cleave and divide proclamation of the Gospel from accompanying miraculous signs and wonders can and is making a distinction and divide that is not accordance with the Word of God?

God the Father, the Son and the Holy Spirit do not always have to reveal their power and authority through the miraculous signs and wonders and yet may be we need to allow for the fact that they can choose at times to do this?

In the Body of Christ today; you either believe in the miraculous signs and wonders and their possibility today or you do not? I believe we need to always leave the door open and allow for the reality that the Godhead can and may act through miraculous signs and wonders? Too often we handcuff the Godhead and seem to believe that they have to dance to our tune rather than acting in any way they want to and can? The God we serve is spirit and can and has and does and will act sovereignly in our Global Village in ways and a way we cannot always reason and even understand?

The One who is the Creator God is allowed to make the rules and to even break them; particularly when they are His creatures intellectual rules and boundaries for His activity in His *creation. We should not box the God who is the Creator God in and mistakenly believe that there are things He cannot do? He is a God who has all power and who can act in ways and through means we do not always understand and can reason through? May well be the God of our imaginations needs to get a whole bigger? It might be that we need to re - configure the way we conceive and view God the Father, the Son and the Holy Spirit?*

We need to resist more and more the temptation to handcuff the God of the universe. He needs to be free to act in any way and fashion according to His character? I hope and pray that the God the Father, the Son and the Holy Spirit and the one of your imagination and reason and intellect just got bigger? May you perceive and come to understand truly the Holy, powerful and majestic Almighty God we serve ....!

4. Healing - is it holistic in its essence, affecting the whole person rather than just their physical bodies?

The question of healing being holistic in its essence is an interesting one to ponder? When somebody is healed in the New Testament context are they just healed in their physical bodies or is there more healing of a holistic nature mind, body, soul and spirit taking place? At times we can become even in our day so focused on physical healing; the healing of broken bodies that we can forget or overlook the other parts that makeup an individual? Mind, body, soul and spirit we all know the divisions of a person but generally too much attention is paid to the physical side of things and the healing of physical bodies?

This is true of Jesus Christ's day and true of our era or epoch in history? People cry out for physical healing; if we have an immediate physical problem causing us pain and even suffering we want it to be healed immediately? True of His time and era and true of our times in today's world?

The problem is that people are not just physical beings with bodies in need of physical healing; they have minds, souls and spirit's also that may be in need of healing as well?

Sometimes it is easy to use a band - aid approach and focus on the person's need for physical healing while forgetting or paying scant attention to the rest of them? Quick - fix and band - aid approaches true both of the medical world and the Body of Christ with regards to healing ministries? In the Body of Christ sometimes it is partly because we are so concerned with seeing the spectacular healing power of God displayed that we can forget about holistic healing and the individual's need for it?

One of the things or concepts or notions that is important to come to terms with is that of ' soaking prayer '. The need to bathe a person who is ill and sick physically in fervent and passionate prayer? In some ways it is like the person takes a bath but does it through the intercessory prayer of another person interceding and praying for their healing. This needs to be consistent prayer that aims to ' soak ' and ' surround ' the person in prayer to God for both their physical healing and the holistic healing of their being mind, body, soul and spirit.

The problem the Body of Christ has is that of time and prayer ministry of this sort taking lots of time. Often more time than just a quick laying - on - of hands in a prayer line at a healing crusade? In the end we need more people in the Body of Christ committed to and operating in and by ' soaking intercessory prayer ministry'.

The primary aim of this sort of prayer ministry will be the holistic healing of the person involved in mind, body, soul and spirit?

The need for prayer for holistic healing of mind, body, soul and spirit is a crying need in the Body of Christ and the Global Village in general. In the early years of medical science there seems to have been more of emphasis on holistic healing. Caring for the whole person mind, body, soul and spirit?

There would appear to

be enough medical evidence to support that when holistic medical care is given and pursued the medical outcomes are better for the individual involved? The same would be true regards holistic prayer ministry in the Body of Christ?

The Hebrew world view deals with the whole person and took a holistic approach to both the individual and the community they were part of? In some ways may be time we remember we were and are created in the ' imago deo ' as whole persons mind, body, soul and spirit? The Greek idea and notion of *a person being sub - divided into their various parts is not and has not always been helpful to both medical science and the Body of Christ?*

More and more I believe we need to see the whole person in front of us and care for them in a holistic fashion? The early New Testament dealt with the issue of healing holistically as well; they cared for and provided for the whole person; not just the person's physical body. We in the so - called Modern Technological Age seem to have lost this emphasis of holistic care for an individual who may be sick and suffering? My hope and prayer is that we may rediscover both the need, want and even desire to pursue both the holistic care of people medically but also in relation to our ministry of prayer to them?

5. Healing and Faith - what role does Faith in Jesus Christ's ability to heal play in obtaining a healing?

The equation we sometimes use or may well be all the time is :
FAITH + HEALING = HEALING OBTAINED .

I am one who believes faith can be important in healing but I do not believe in ' faithing it ' to your healing? The Father, the Son and the Holy Spirit have all knowledge and power and they may not heal? I and you cannot twist their arms and get them to bring healing into an individual's life? At times we have to live with the reality that at different times healing does not always happen or take place in the way or ways we want?

In the New Testament accounts people got healed by Jesus Christ even when they did not have faith in both their healing or in Jesus Christ? Given this then; I do not believe that healing and it not happening is because of a lack of faith? Some people in the Body of Christ always go there and

' blame the victim ' and their apparent lack of faith? It is too easy to do and does not help anybody involved in terms of the person's family or the wider Body of Christ? We like to believe its a bit like ' pin the tail on the donkey ' and that we can always nail down why healing has not taken place in a person's life? Its too easy to do this and it is a trap that many fall into; ' the so - called blame game '.

As we look at the faith shown by the Royal Official in the word and words of Jesus Christ regarding the healing of his son; we can be amazed at such faith being shown? While it may not have been the faith the Official showed in the word and words of Jesus Christ that led ultimately to the healing of his son it is yet important to see it for what it is?

Healing as we have already noted can take place despite and in the face of a lack of faith in it and in Jesus Christ on the part of the one seeking the healing? The other thing to note is that much like the faith that Jesus Christ ' saw ' as the friends lowered their friend through the roof is also important to understand as well? Our faith for an individual who is in pain, suffering and in need of healing; can and does have an important role to play; we can stand in the gap and believe for another person and their healing? Our faith can be and will be honored and used and energized by Jesus Christ. Our faith in the face of somebodies physical need is not inert and of no value; our faith can and does have impact and effect and can have positive consequences for the person in need of healing? Jesus Christ can see our faith for the person who needs healing and He can honor our faith? What Jesus chooses to do with our faith regards their healing is His sovereign choice? There is always the possibility that He can bring physical healing to the person?

In some way and ways I do not fully understand faith and even our own faith is the ' currency of heaven '? The faith and our faith for the healing of the person in the front of us has an important role and function to play? May we be more like the Royal Official at show real faith in the word and words of Jesus Christ in terms of the holistic healing of people's minds, bodies,souls and spirits?

John 4 : 46 - 54 CEB

" He returned to Cana in Galilee where he had turned the water into wine. In Capernaum there was a certain royal official whose son was sick.

When he heard that Jesus was coming from Judea to Galilee, he went out to meet him and asked Jesus if he would come and heal his son, for his son was about to die.

Jesus said to him, " Unless you see miraculous signs and wonders, you won't believe."

The royal official said to him,

"Lord, come before my son dies."

Jesus replied, "Go home. Your son lives." The man believed the word that Jesus spoke to him and set out for his home.

While he was on his way, his servants were already coming to meet him. They said, "Your son lives."

So he asked them at what time his son had started to get better. And they said, "The fever left him yesterday at about one o'clock in the afternoon."

Then the father realized that this was the hour when Jesus had said to him, "Your son lives." And he and his entire household believed in Jesus.

This was the second miraculous sign Jesus did while going from Judea to Galilee."

6. The lessons we can and should learn from John 4 : 46 - 54 ?

The first lesson to learn from the text of John 4 : 46 - 54 is that the Royal Official came boldly to Jesus Christ. The Official came to Jesus Christ with his need and the need of his dying son for healing boldly and without any form of pretense or ' airs and graces ' ? He knows why he wants to come to Jesus Christ; he has heard of what Jesus had been doing? He comes with some form of expectation that his dying can receive healing from Jesus Christ?

In his boldness and wanton

abandon in seeking out Jesus for the healing of his son; the Official is showing a lot of faith, trust and even ultimately belief in Jesus Christ? So often in the Body of Christ we do not come boldly before Jesus with our requests for our healing or someone else's healing? We rather unlike the Royal Official, hang back in the shadows of life and act and behave as if we would believe and have faith if we could; may be we will have faith and show or may be we will not? At times it is like we reluctantly agree to have faith and belief in Jesus Christ and His desire to bring healing; if only He would give us some reason or sign that leads to it? Pre - preemptive healing , a sign , a glimmer of the foreshadowed healing and the healing we want to see take place?

As Hebrews states we can boldly come before the throne of grace through the blood and sacrifice of Jesus Christ to obtain grace and mercy? The question I have for you is why do we not do that; that is to come before the throne of grace boldly? We have more reason to do this boldly; come before the throne of grace boldly given that we are living post - cross of Jesus Christ? Jesus Christ has been crucified, died, buried and risen again from the dead. We can come before the throne of grace boldly; we are allowed to, we have access - all - areas; his death, burial and resurrection is our guarantee of access? So why not come boldly before the throne of grace and obtain the grace and mercy you need or somebody you know needs in the form of physical healing?

The other lesson from the text is that the faith and belief that the Royal Official displayed was also accompanied by action on his part. He did not just believe or have faith in the *word of Jesus Christ it was ' faith - in - action '. His departure to return to his dying son; demonstrates his very real faith and belief in the word of healing for his son that Jesus had spoken?*

So often in the Body of Christ we can be given words or a word from Jesus Christ and we do not have or pursue a corresponding action that demonstrates our faith or belief in the word or words given? The word or words we can be given from Jesus Christ fall to the ground and are not accepted, actualized and become realities in our lives. May well be because we do not trust Him to honor His word or words to us? This has been true in my own life and I do not believe I am alone in it? Inaction and a lack of response in the face of a word or words over my life from Jesus Christ is sometimes the hallmark of my life and response to the word given? At all times we need to trust in the author of the word or words of both healing and otherwise given by Jesus Christ to us? This is true even in the face of doubt, opposition and persecution we need to have faith and belief in the One who spoke the word or words to us; Jesus Christ?

The final lesson I want to draw out of the text is that the positive outcome in terms of the healing of his son generated an even more faithful response from the Official and his entire household. The result of the physical healing of his son, was for Him and his household (oikos) to come to believe in and have faith in Jesus Christ. The interesting aspect to understand is that the Official just wanted physical healing for his dying son; he was not there because he wanted to come to faith in Jesus Christ?

So often we see people come to Jesus Christ wanting Him to heal, restore and bless them in some way and they come in the end to faith and belief in Jesus Christ? I believe Jesus Christ is both concerned with the immediate physical need and needs of the people involved but He also has a regard for the eternal destiny of them as well? I believe this is eloquently demonstrated by the narrative and text we have been considering? Both the immediate physical of the man's son were met as well as their eternal destinies?

At times it is like ' the chicken and the egg; ' which comes first the chicken or the egg? Both the chicken and the egg are important and have a part to play and both are affected in some ways by circumstances? The miracle of healing happens for the Official's son and that generates faith and belief in the whole of his household. The very real question is sometimes what is more important; the immediate - in - your - face physical need and reality or the eternal destiny question and need? I believe in a Jesus Christ who is concerned about both and who does want to alleviate the physical pain and suffering of an individual in real - time? For me it is all tied up with the compassion, love and care for the individual who had a need for physical healing I read about in the pages of the New Testament? Jesus Christ does still care, love and have compassion upon the physical infirmities people have and He understand the physical realities they live with. He is not a God who does not care and is impassible (without emotions)?

I believe Jesus Christ who intercedes and intervenes in His creatures lives. The in - breaking of *the supernatural power of God in healing comes out of the very compassionate beating of the heart of God the Father, the Son and the Holy Spirit. For physical healing and even as we have dealt with in holistic healing of a person's life springs from the heart of God................ So the question is why do we sometimes believe that God wants to do damage and wreak havoc and disaster in our lives and not heal holistically and physically? As we have already noted sometimes we both handcuff God and also imagine Him as being far smaller than He really is? May well our image and way and ways of picturing the God we serve has to grow and change?*

EPILOGUE :

Word and words from Jesus Christ in John 4 : 46 - 54; the Royal Official believes the word and words of Jesus Christ. We need to trust the word and words of Jesus Christ to ourselves and others; particularly in terms of physical healing and holistic healing for people?

We saw how there is a need for the healing people receive to be holistic? At times we can be so concerned with physical healing that we can forget and overlook the rest of the person. There is a need for ' soaking prayer ' ministry which has at its heart a concern for the holistic healing of an individual's life?

The great thing we

came to see from the text was the amazing faith and belief of the Royal Official in Jesus Christ's desire and ability to bring healing to his dying son. There is a need for those in the wider Body of Christ to emulate the faith and belief of the Official. We need to trust and believe in Jesus Christ's ability, desire and intention to bring physical healing and holistic healing to those we pray for.

Finally, we talked about the ' Chicken and the egg' and how the healing of the Official's dying son led ultimately to salvation for his whole household? The question is always both what is more important and what should come first in the scheme of things? I affirmed my own belief in a Jesus Christ who is full of love, care and compassion for the physical realities people face and their need for physical healing at different times in their lives? Physical healing and holistic healing is still on the table and it should remain important to us in the Body of Christ because it comes out of the very heart of God, the Father, the Son and the Holy Spirit?

AMEN and AMEN.
Shalom........

Lightning Source UK Ltd.
Milton Keynes UK
UKHW051152020619
343606UK00005B/126/P

9 781366 486516